SARAH

Quand Même

A new play created pour le centieme
anniversaire of the death of Sarah Bernhardt.

by Susie Lindeman

Published by Playdead Press 2024

© Susie Lindeman 2024

Susie Lindeman has asserted her rights under the Copyright, Design and Patents Act, 1988, to be identified as the author of this work.

A CIP catalogue record for this book is available from the British Library.

ISBN 978-1-915533-23-4

Playdead Press
www.playdeadpress.com

Sarah, Quand Meme was created for the centenary of Sarah Bernhardt's death, when almost a million Parisians took to the streets in 28th March 1923.

The world premiere took place at le Théâtre de Nèsle, Paris on 28th March 2023.

The Australian premiere took place at the Meraki Arts Mainstage, Sydney in Aug 2023.

The British premiere season took place at the Drayton Arms Theatre, London from 20th February – 2nd March 2024.

The cast and creative were as follows.

CAST:
Sarah / Lysiane | **Susie Lindeman**
Maurice (voice) | **Patrick Toomey**

CREATIVE:
Writer & Performer | **Susie Lindeman**
Director & Dramaturg | **Wayne Harrison**
Lighting Designer | **Martin Kinnane**
Production Designer | **Justin Nardella**
Stage Manager | **Lauren Madden**

Susie Lindeman | Writer and Performer

Susie's stage credits include: *Six Characters In Search of An Author* (Sydney Opera House); *Sons Of Cain; The Admirable Crichton; Prin* and *The Deep Blue Sea* (West End). Other stage credits include: *Cosi; A Dolls House; L'Aide-Memoire; Hilda; Hammerklavier (by and as Yasmina Reza); Madame Melville; 4.48 Psychosis; The Marvelous Boy; Paris Letter; Sweet Phoebe; Poster Girl; The Marriage Of Figaro; The Imaginary Invalid; Prevail* and *Happy As Larry And Viv.*

Susie originated the role of Vivien Leigh in *Letter To Larry* by Donald Macdonald (*Paris, London, Atlanta*).

Screen credits include: Oscar/BAFTA winning *Howards End;* the Prix Europa winning *Catherine;* Penguin Award winning *Palace of Dreams; Melba; Robbery Under Arms; Maigret* (opposite Michael Gambon); *Let Them Eat Cake* (with French and Saunders) and *Top Of The Lake* (for Jane Campion).

As Writer, her first play *Persephone ("Greek myth a hit!"* SMH) was also adapted for screen, winning Gold for Best Independent at the Charleston International Film Festival. *SARAH Quand Même* is Susie's third play, following *A gap E.* Her screenplays include: *Passe Partout; A***Memoire* and *Viv...*

Wayne Harrison AM | Director & Dramaturg

Wayne is the former Director / CEO of Sydney Theatre Company where he directed over 50 productions, including the award-*winning Into the Woods; Shadowlands; Two Weeks with the Queen* and David Williamson's *Dead White Males.*

Recent theatre credits include: *Mom's the Word: Talkin' Turkey* (Arts Club Theatre Vancouver, with a return season 2023); *The One Day of the Year* (Finborough Theatre, London

& Live Stream); *Letter to Larry (*Theatre de Nesle, Paris & the *Gone With the Wind* Festival in Atlanta, Georgia); *Human Nature – The Motown Show* & *Jukebox* (The Venetian, Las Vegas); and *Coming of Age in Australia* (School of Drama, Flinders University SA).

As the Head of Creation for Spiegelworld International, productions Wayne has written and directed include: *Absinthe; Desir, Empire* (New York); *Vegas Nocturne* (Las Vegas) and *Absinthe* (Miami and Las Vegas). His production of *Absinthe* at Caesar's Palace in Las Vegas is now in its thirteenth year.

Martin Kinnane | Lighting Designer

Martin designs lighting for theatre and events both in Australia and internationally. A NIDA Graduate, he has worked extensively with the Ensemble Theatre, Hothouse, White Box, Griffin, and Bell Shakespeare, and commercial tours of *Alone It Stands* and *Defending the Caveman*.

International credits include *Desir* and *Absinthe* for Speigelworld (New York and Miami); *Letter to Larry* and *Sarah: Quand Meme* (Theatre de Nesle in Paris).

Martin is best known for his lighting designs for all City of Sydney's New Year's Eve events between 2001-2007. His spectacularly theatrical lighting of the Sydney Harbour Bridge (the Bridge Effect) has brought him international renown.

Justin Nardella | Production Designer

Justin is a London based Set and Costume designer working in stage, screen and special events. A NIDA graduate, involved in productions around the globe, from award-winning fringe shows to West End residencies and international tours, including *Jean-Paul Gaultier's Fashion Freak Show* (its London season and tours to Japan and Germany), plus Deborah Warner's production of *Peter Grimes* for the Royal Opera House, London and *Songs For Nobodies* in London's West End. He has collaborated with some of the worlds leading companies and professionals to bring stories to life.

REVIEWS:

Mesmerizing performance... not to be missed. ...towering tour-de-force... embracing an astonishing life and destiny.
Francois Pier Pelinard. Paris

Drama finely cut... There is magic to the ending Susie Lindeman brings to the enthralling portrayal of the life, achievement, doubts and aspirations of a performer who was in a league of her own. This performance too was in a league of its own. Her eyes dazzle, mesmerising the audience in a language of their own. It is almost as if Lindeman channels Bernhardt, in all her charm, pathos, intensity, craft and intelligence. The audience was transported into another world and time, as fresh as the sunshine of the day just past. At the heart of the show is an antiquarian brilliance that continues to shine a universal truth one century after it was first extinguished.
Sydney Arts Guide

Susie Lindeman, as the writer and actor, does not so much perform the role, but more so inhabits the very core of the character. A fascinating insight into a superstar
StageWhispers

The writer would like to acknowledge her research materials: 'Sarah Bernhardt, My Grandmother' by Lysiane Bernhardt, 'Up In the Clouds', 'Ma Double Vie' by Sarah Bernhardt, and the program for her Australian tour.

Sarah was always somehow known to me, but in exploring her power of the feminine I discovered Sarah's greatest strength was in being human- way ahead of her time. Susie Lindeman

Dedicated to my mother, Jill Lindeman

In appreciation of Yasmina Reza and Jean-Claude Carrière, for their professional and personal inspiration, merci.

With Thanks to:
Shauna Wilson, Associate Producer, Persophia
Catherine Davray, Agence Davray, Paris
Jemma Redgrave; Pamela Carsaniga; Audrey Thaner.

And
Wayne Harrison, for his vision, care and contribution in bringing SARAH Quand Même from the page to the stage.

CHARACTERS:

Sarah – the great actress, 50s and future

Lysiane – her granddaughter, 13 and future

Maurice – Sarah's son

Both Sarah and Lysiane are to be played by the same actress

SETTING:

In Sarah's dressing room and salon at home.

Upstage:
A chaise-lounge, laid with a long travelling fur, beside a small table with crystal ball and tarot cards, a petite carafe of white port and glass.

Stage right:
A dressing table area and mirror lights.

Stage left:
A single chair (initially covered by a leopard skin coat)

There are cream coloured pages laid out in a spiral on the floor centre-stage, which both the characters pick up and use.

TIME:

The time shifts between 1890s – 1923

NOTE:

Italics in the dialogue denote quotes from a play

Music fades in. Lights low.

Sarah, dressed in flowing white layers à la dame aux camellias, enters, steps the spiral of pages, then turns upstage and lays on the chaise-longue to sleep.

Music fades over. Lights slowly fade in over the chaise-longue.

Sound of a thud.

Sarah wakes, and rises with the lines from her dream.

SARAH: '*Etre ou ne pas être...*
          ça, c'est la question.
          To be... or not to be? That is the question
          And the answer...?

          Hamlet had only two choices, but a woman

She considers.

          Il y a trois actes à l'intérieur d'une femme;

          Feeling... Fight... Flight

Lights slowly fill downstage.

She steps downstage and circles the spiral of pages, considering.

          Yes, I've played men...but have I played as a
          man?
          The roles were never primarily masculine they
          were human...

She stops and turns inside the central spiral

          Their feminine principle was closer... intuition,
          emotion...

This was the drama. Ça, ç'est la drame

She leaps into a pose, raising her arm as if holding a fencing foil.

Oui, je joue Hamlet… and…

She pauses, then suddenly she cups her hands and calls out front, as Lysiane, Sarah's granddaughter

LYSIANE: You are the only Ophelia to do so Grandmère!

Sarah looks into the auditorium

SARAH: Oh Lysiane! What a naughty little granddaughter.
You know better than to interrupt my warm up on stage!
Come down! And you know well not to call me *Grandmère* in a theatre.

Just call me 'Grande'

And *I sincerely hope your destiny has more exciting prospects than standing about waiting for me.'*

LYSIANE: Ha, the only Hamlet to play Phèdre!

Sound of thud

SARAH: Ah, nearly showtime.

She turns towards the dressing-room then back as Lysiance.

LYSIANE: Non, it's story time! You said you'd tell me a true story, with a beginning, middle and end. You promised.

11

SARAH: Will you write it down?

LYSIANE: Avec plaisir Grand… Grande

SARAH: Bon, but just the beginning.

            Alors, I began… because my mother was a
            (*spelling it out*)

            C.O.U.R.T.E.S.A.N

            And when she wasn't abandoning me, leaving
            me to the cleaning lady for years.

Lays out on the chaise longue

            Maman lay on her sofa and didn't know what to
            do with me.
            I was trouble. (*sitting up*) Even as a baby, left
            alone in my high-chair, I pull the peg from the
            lock and… fall straight into a flaming fire.
            I was covered in butter for months, until I
            became new.
            In my skin. Dans mon peau… Dans moi.

            Maman finally came home. Elle m'a regardée,
            mais elle ne m'a jamais vue.
            She never saw the me inside.
            Je suis seule.
            Because Maman loved my little sisters, Jeanne
            and Regina, much more than me, I was sent to
            the Convent Grands Champs, Versailles. I am
            five.

*She takes off her robe, revealing a simple child's dress, and
crosses herself to kneel.*

Holy Mary, Mother of God, pray for me and I,
Sarah, will play for you.

I will paint and make clay models... ooh I love
the smell of incense, the Catholic rituals. Oh, I
want to become a nun!

Standing quickly, serieuse

So what if I'm Jewish?

Let me play Raphael in *Tobias and the Angel*
when the Archbishop of Paris visits. You said I
have 'heavenly eyes'?

She wanders as a child.

Non. There is no role for me, Lysiane, even
though I know every line. Until the chubby
'chosen one' falls into fits of terror in the wings,
and they beg me to go on and save the show!

She quickly steps into 'the stage' area of the spiral.

Je suis une ange!
And the convent dog played the sea-monster.

She looks deep into the auditorium.

Le monstre...

She slowly steps back

On the eve of my 14th birthday, my mother said
'tonight, Sarah, we are taking you to la Comédie
Française'.
I *scowled*. But inside I was thrilled...

My mother's friend, the Duc de Mornay winked.
He knew my mother's despair of me, declaring
'Only the theatre could give that girl a future.
White gloves'. Oui, mon oncle.

She quickly finds and puts on white gloves and looks around the
salle

The Duc's carriage. La salle de la Comédie
Française, the royal box!
Le programme. *(sits)* Les lumières.

Lights change as if in a theatre

La pièce commence... and the magic begins.
Et moi, j'entre çe nouveau monde. The actors
move me.
Their words *This city and your mother are desolate*
of you I don't understand, but les comédiens me
touchent, their characters fill me up
Au point des larmes, *(to tears)*
By the interval I am sobbing.
Maman is chatting with friends, whilst my arms
and head rest on the velvet edge of the box.
Sobbing alone.
The audience below turn to look up at me.
As one, comme un... *monstre.* Avec mille des
visages.
I stare back, tears dripping.
These thousand faces, their shocked eyes,
frowning furrows, whispered words. Captivés
I lean over so they can see me better, and sob a
little more.

14

(*whispering*)

> Bonsoir (*wiping her tears*)
> Mon monstre bien aimé .
> I am seen for the very first time. Je suis vue,
> pour la première fois.

Glancing hopefully to her 'mother'

> But my mother doesn't see me...
> Still, the Duc tells her I must enter le
> Conservatoire
> I prepare my audition

Tearing the 'program' into two pages and considering them.

> Un extrait de comédie
> Et un d'un tragédie.
> But... I don't know what to learn. I only
> know...

Sound of bell

She flings the pages into the air and hurries downstage to recite

> Two Pigeons, a fable, reçit de Sarah Bernhardt.
> Mais, j'ai le trac... I'm shaking.
> *Deux Pigeons s'aimaient d'amour tendre.*
> My face, swollen from tears of fear,
> Burst into blushes.
> *L'un d'eux s'ennuyant au logis*

Sound of bell

> They cage my two pigeons after only two lines.
> *Attends... Qu'allez-vous faire?*

15

Sound of bell

> I forget to breathe and faint in my final
> competition

She falls back on the chaise-longue

> Et the winner is... pas moi. Not me.
> Second prize? Sarah Bernhardt!
> But my mother was appalled; 'Now you shall
> forever be the loser'.
> She wanted me gone. And I wanted to go...
>
> But I wanted most to tame the monster. I knew
> from the convent about absolute self-sacrifice,
> renunciation, devotion. I would use them to
> become an actress. It was an overwhelming
> feeling.

She puts the robe back on.

> But when I was your age, Lysiane, it was
> forbidden to feel.
> So I was drilled in the classic style, the
> Alexandrines, the given gesture.
> Guided not to freely move my body. (*turning her
> lithe body like a free art deco dancer*). Like this,
> and this, or this!
> Am I good, bad, celebrated or cursed?

She stops.

> The monster will decide, Lysiane. When you
> write this story... as a book.
> You have the notes and quotes? Look.

She picks up a page from the spiral of pages on the floor

LYSIANE: Oui, ma grande, of how you broke through

Sarah flourishes the page and steps away.

SARAH: And broke every rule. My classmates were cruel.

"Ooh, her arms are too long! Il y a une puce dans sa robe!

Non, il y'en a deux! *(touching her chest)* Look, there are two fleas in her dress! She has no flesh, how can she play a lover, this scarecrow!'

They hated me.

LYSIANE: But they love your 'golden voice.'

SARAH: Not yet "You have a pretty voice, but we cannot hear you. PROJECT!"
They gave me a scene from Voltaire. And tell me I must denounce "*Strike him down! I love him*" with violence. Ah bon? But surely this is a moment about facing death, a softness... Non, AVEC VIOLENCE Mademoiselle.
Bon, I nod. But when I come to the moment, I find I am so truly broken, and my heart is truly trembling and I can only utter a very real sob for '*Strike him down, I love him*' (*Collapsing, she peeks up*).
Was I terrible?

Sound of applause.

Non, Lysiane... it is all quickening and repose.

17

> Story of my life.
> Not just the story of the shows

Sound of thud –
Stage lights on
She steps into performance on 'the stage' area.

> *These gods are my witnesses, these gods who place*
> *The fire in my breast, fatale to my race.*
> *Ces dieux qui se sont fait une gloire cruelle*
> *Des séduire le coeur d'une faible mortelle.*

Applause

Stage lights off

A moment. Sarah recovers, and wipes tears.

LYSIANE: Grandmère, tu pleures?

SARAH: Non, these are the tears of Phedre. It is she who conquers the stage, not I.

LYSIANE: But it is you Grandmère who conquered the world.

SARAH: I *questioned* the world. Europe, L'Amerique, même L'Australie, mais ils vont m'oublier.

LYSIANE: No, they won't forget. (*Picking up a page and reading)*"When all of genius that can perish dies, the memory of Sarah Bernhardt's Marguerite Gautier in La Dame Aux Camellias will not fade away…"

SARAH: Even in a hundred years?

LYSIANE: 'Rare emotional art by which genius gives all truth'...

'Despair and exquisite delicacy of Madame Bernhardt's style will last forever.

Sarah fans herself with the page in her hand.

SARAH: Delicacy, delicacy. Once, when I perform Marguerite I saw Eleanor Duse – some say the second best actress in the world – in the 2nd row, dressed in her costume as Marguerite from when she made a success in the role. I curtsy, delicately.

Then I have an affair with her lover, I was curious!

Vas-y, Lysiane read on.

She sits on the chaise-longue and Lysiane reaches down to get a new page

LYSIANE: 'I have never seen a more comical figure than Sarah when she appears in a simple dress, and yet one soon stops laughing, for every inch of that little figure lives and bewitches... flattering, imploring, embracing... incredible postures every limb and joint acts with her. A curious being.
I can imagine that she needn't be any different in life than on the stage'

SARAH: Who said that?

LYSIANE: DH Lawrence.

SARAH: Never met him.

But Sigmund Freud kept a picture of me in his office, whether to inspire or warn, who knows... and George Bernard Shaw... (*looking down at the page*) "Her acting is not the art of making you think more highly or more deeply but the art of making you admire her, pity her, champion her, weep with her, laugh at her jokes, follow her fortunes breathlessly and applaud her wildly when the curtain falls... It is the art of fooling you"

Non. (*She is hurt*) It is the art of 'feeling' for you.

I never fake it. Well, perhaps there were one or two lovers who...

LYSIANE: The Prince of Wales?

SARAH: Pas du tout, he was... but you are much to young to know.

LYSIANE: I am more than 13!

SARAH: Well, I never fake it on stage!

Sound of thud

Nearly Showtime.

She stands. Lysiane looks for a page.

LYSIANE: Not yet. Finish the beginning of how you joined at La Comédie Française

SARAH: I was invited to audition, but… would they like me?

She looks into the auditorium and smiles, hopefully. Then steps back in rejection.

Non… Trop mince, trop étranger
Trop de trop.

She sits on the chaise-longue, deflated, dropping the page.

Only Marie Lloyd, who won first prize at the Conservatoire when I won second, was kind. I study how she smoothes her dress with a serenity I have never known. Me, I wept in my final scene so my nose was running. The judges dismissed me for having a cold!

She lays back.

They will never take me, my mother was convinced.
But (*spying a page on the floor, she jumps up to read it*) the next morning a letter arrives with an official invitation to join the company! My mother signed quickly!

She steps with great pride to the dressing-room.

And in my first dressing-room I take my greasepaint to the mirror and I write:

She writes the words in the air

'Quand Même!'

LYSIANE: Your motto.

SARAH: My *vow*. The English cannot make a straight translation. 'When even'? (*laughs*) Non! 'Despite all', No Matter What!'

She touches the words in the air, then gathers a script and heads to centre-stage.

And in my first rehearsal, I meet a man called the 'director?' who tells me I cannot have the moon shining for my moment.

She steps downstage

But, I explain to him, showing him the script, it says 'she is pale and distressed in the rays of the moon'.
Alors, I am pale and distressed. And I just need my moon, Monsieur.
"J'ai dit non, Mademoiselle Bernhardt, you cannot have the moon!
The leading actress, the tall and voluptuous Sophie Croizette, must have the moon. She will kiss in its light. Her beauty will be captured / "
/ But I need the moon too! Pour la texte. Aren't we serving the playwright?
Perhaps I stamp my foot and I am told to go to my dressing room.

She does, troubled

Then they send me home.

She paces, troubled.

For two days I am not called to rehearsal, but on the third day I return…

She steps centre-stage

> I walk onstage, there is no director.
> I look up, voilà, il y a deux lunes.
> You see, Lysiane, two moons.
> Quand même!

Lysiane suddenly claps.

LYSIANE: But you are the *only* sun in the sky! Dona Sol. Especially when you took off in that hot air balloon and flew from Paris to Brittany before an evening show!

SARAH: You exaggerate, Lysiane

LYSIANE: Non, ma Grande, it's all in the novella you wrote: *Dans Les Nuages* about

Lights up on chair

> *(She quickens to the chair and pulls off the leopard skin coat)* The little chair that went up in a hot air balloon. And a Great Actress went too.

SARAH: But the little chair tells the story.

Lysiane leaps into the chair

LYSIANE: I loved you reading it to me 'The great actress's lovely voice conquered my heart' exclaimed the chair.

Sarah takes on the story, sitting more sedately down.

23

SARAH: But, the chair also confessed... 'One day I heard a stout gentleman who sat on me heap insult upon insult;

She's so dreadfully affected.

She would do anything to get attention!

She has no acting talent whatsoever!

She keeps someone hidden backstage to speak her roles and merely supplies the gestures!'

Lysiane spritely rises up onto the seat of the chair and continues the story

LYSIANE: 'She keeps a starving sculptor locked in a closet who is really responsible for the figures she claims to model'.

'And as for her painting...! Does she even know how to hold a brush?!!

She laughs and unbalances

And the mean man was jostled by the chair, and fell to his fat derriere!

She falls off the chair

I loved that little chair. You took it home

She stands and Sarah touches the chair gently.

SARAH: Yes, to give it a place of honour. To give me strength.

You see I was still nervous, especially for the tour to London. La Comédie Française had a reputation to uphold.

She whispers

Quand meme, quand même

She wanders centre stage.

When we arrived in England Lysiane, oh la la.
The crowds, the chaos… A red carpet was lain
along the dock and to the train platform. It was
thrilling for the company to see so many people.
But, someone explains, the fanfare was for the
Prince and Princess of Wales, just departed for
France.

I am crushed.

Crushed between Croizette and the others, and I
nearly fall.

But a man's hand steadies me.

A tall young man, with a poet's style, smiles.

"You should have a carpet of flowers,
Mademoiselle" and he tosses the lilies he
clutches to the ground.

I step forward and everyone steps away. The
man calls out.

"That the great Comedie Francaise arrives is
already an event, but to also bring the great
Sarah B, whom I now name 'La Divine', is a
sensation!

He takes off his hat. "I am Oscar Wilde".

And the company was wild with jealousy.

She relives her surprise.

> They program me to perform just the second
> Act of Phedre, during… interval?

> A teaser, because I have been singled out, to
> triumph or to tear me down?

She moves to the Dressing Room

SARAH: Opening night, I was terrified.
No First Act to warm up in, to thread Phedre
through my psyche.
Non, I must dive deep into the dramatic scene.
Straight in, bang!

Looking in the 'mirror.'

> I do my make up a million times, blackened
> eyes, pale powder, I look dreadful and I am
> shaking.

She moves 'on stage.'

> I enter the stage to the sound of muttering, so I
> must raise my voice.

> *Tout mon sang vers mon coeur se retire*

> Oh, merde, I've started too high. I cannot lower
> my voice now, I must continue. Quand Même.

> *These gods are my witnesses, these gods who place*
> *The fire in my breast, so fatale to my race*
> *Présente je vous fuis, absente je vous trouve*

26

Dans le font des forêts votre image me suit.

I spy some actors sniggering in the wings, and I decide to fly.

Grâce au ciel, mes mains ne sont point criminelles. Plût aux dieux que mon coeur fût innocent comme elles.

She stops. Glancing into the audience.

Some of the audience return from the bar, and stand in the aisles. Cheering
This monster loves me?
I stare through the glinting light spots and see Henry Irving- the greatest actor of all leading the applause. Oh!
I was enthralled with London. I felt I had been let out of a cage.

She sits, opening her arms in joy, on the chaise-longue.

LYSIANE: (*teasing*) Like a lioness.

SARAH: Ah! It was no secret that I wanted a lion. I had an exhibition, sold 10 of my paintings and 6 sculptures my paintings to have enough money. But life doesn't give us what we think we want. Instead –

LYSIANE: – you buy a cheetah that becomes famous too.

SARAH: Infamous. It just happened that a London journalist came to see me 'Ah, Madame Bernhardt again dressed in white and her figure so willow wispy'

Hmm.

Come into the garden, *(under her breath)* You can
meet my cheetah

It bounds towards us, bedlam in the flowerbeds.

She collects the fallen fur coat, stroking it as if it were a cheetah

I turn to the Journalist's horrified face.
Mais c'est normal. J'adore les animaux. I take
this one for walks in Hyde Park, but of course I
leave my lynx, wolves, boa constrictor and
alligator at home. Ah, you see his collar is made
of diamonds. Would you like to stroke him and
hear him purr?

Glancing up, the journalist has run away.

Monsieur?

I didn't tell him I was penniless. Keeping a
menagerie costs money.
Despite 42 performances earning the company
millions, I am the least paid actress at the
Comédie Française, so I perform privately in
salons, avec les Anglais.

She wraps the fur around her shoulders and applauds

Oh, how Ellen Terry inspires me. She's the
beloved embodiment of Victorian femininity, an
unmarried mother of two, and Henry Irving's
lover! She calls me 'Sally B'!

And that's when Beatrice Stella first casts her
spell on me – but why do they insist on calling
her 'Mrs. Patrick Campbell'?
As if her *husband* gives her identity!

*She tosses the fur to the chaise-longue, then turns back,
considering.*

Though it's true, Lysiane, when I later play her
husband on stage, I *do* get first billing, *Pelleas* et
Melisande.
And I met Millais!

She steps back to sit on the chaise-longue

Oui, the great pre-Raphaelite artist sat next to
me at dinner.
Diving into Ophelia's brook with him. *(laying
back)*
The watery grave… the petals paling the death
of hope, the hope of death.
(sitting up) I ask him, do you think Gertrude
watched Ophelia drown?
She describes every detail so clearly, and it
sounds so peaceful.

She stares for a moment, then busily resumes her story.

Oh, that reminds me, Lysiane, I need to tell you
why the coffin.

LYSIANE: The one in your bedroom?

SARAH: Oui, ç'est très simple. Après le conservatoire, I
nearly died, and for 6 weeks I coughed up blood

29

then lay unconscious. The doctors said 'Elle va mourir, elle est trop faible'. They advised my mother to arrange a coffin.

I did not need it, but please Maman, let me keep it.

This white satin-lined resting place becomes a sanctuary… a place of recovery. And discovery.

LYSIANE: It's where you read your scripts, I know.

SARAH: Reading, thinking and *feeling*, from being still, yet still alive.

I only ever slept in it when my baby sister Regina was so very ill and needed my bed.

She takes a moment.

But one morning my manicurist arrived early to find me in it and ran to tell the press. So my innocent escape became an escapade in the eyes of Paris society.

They started to think me crazy.

And one time, so did I.

She stands, uncomfortable at the memory.

I confess Lysiane, that once I forgot some lines. It was opium /

LYSIANE: Grandmère!

She moves to the dressing-room

SARAH: Administered to me by a doctor for my nerves an hour before the show.

The play was *L'Etrangère*, and I did feel very
strange
I fainted three times in the dressing room, but
they let me go on.

She moves to the stage area, playing it out.

The first act was misty and my feet glided... but
it went well.
The second act? I don't remember, but...
In the third act, just as I am about to tell
Croizette's character all the detailed troubles of
my character's life I...

Rien. I remember nothing.

She stares at 'Croizette'.

Croizette gives me my first line, which I cannot
hear, and only see her lips moving. But I am
calm, terribly calm and can hear myself say,
quite lucidly "The reason I sent for you Madame
is to tell you all my reasons for acting as I have
done... so many reasons... I must tell you all of
them...

But... but... but

She waits for the lines, then makes a decision

I have thought it over and have decided not to
tell you this, not today"

She holds her ground.

> Croizette stares at me and turns on her heel to
> exit the stage.

Sarah hurries towards the wings to see what's happening there.

> Backstage is buzzing:
> "What happened, Croizette? What's the matter?
> "Sarah is mad! She has cut her entire scene with
> me!"
> They peer at me, their terrified faces hidden
> from the audience.

She turns slowly back to her audience.

> 200 lines cut.

She crosses the stage, commanding her choice.

> But this was London and my monster didn't
> notice anything was wrong.
> Coquelin enters to end the show.
> And the curtain comes down early.

Applause

She curtseys and slowly rises.

> Ooh, I have made a fantastic discovery.
> What is *not* said resonates more.
> If we use instinct to think as our character
> would but not spell it out.
> Ç'est formidable! But the company was furious.
> They see me now as a wild animal loose in the
> house of Moliere!
>
> This, Lysiane was the beginning of the end...

My wings were itching.
Monsieur Wilde is writing a new play.
Ç'est pour moi, çette 'Salome?'
A new page. A new chapter.

She picks up a page for Lysiane who considers it.

LYSIANE: 'The Beginning of the End. The Middle?'

SARAH: Oui... Those last weeks in London the English
press were following the Paris tirade. I was being
cancelled.

She moves to the dressing-room.

So, I spoke to a very fine actress, Madeleine
Brohan, who I looked up to.
Such a gentle heart, I thought she would say all
is well.
She took my face in her hands, and studied me.
'My poor dear, you can do nothing to prevent
this'.
Ah bon? She turned my head to the mirror to
see if she could find a better angle.

Each look at her reflection in the mirror.

'You are original, without trying to be'.
I slip from her grasp.

'Madeleine' continues.

'Dreadful head of hair and your slenderness is
exaggerated
And as for that special voice, it is considered a
certain treason'.

33

Sarah is hurt

Oh!

'Madeleine' doesn't notice

'Anyway, that's what's the matter with you
physically.'
'Now, for your moral defects. You cannot hide
your thoughts, you cannot stoop, you cannot
accept compromise. So you cannot expect not
to arouse jealousy and spite'

I want to go.
'Attends'

*Madeleine looks into Sarah's reflection in the dressing-table
mirror*

'If you are discouraged by these attacks it will
be all over for you with no strength to withstand
them.
So, I advise you to brush your hair
To lose your girlish figure and let you voice
break occasionally
Then you would annoy no one.

Or, *if* you wish to remain yourself, prepare for
injustice and place it at the foundation of your
pedestal.'

Sarah slowly steps away

Was she right? Will I never be accepted?

I had looked at her with envy- but now I realize
her calm is because she has no spirit, no
positivity.

She turns back

Except that she's positively fat, and no one
mentions that!
Such plumpness in her cheeks could she even *see*
me?
Just like Maman!

She stops, in horror

I march home, arming myself for the struggle.

Striding the spiral of pages.

With every step I vow to die in the midst of
battle, rather than regret any failure at the end
of my life!

Sound of thud

She stops. Filled with fire.

So, I shall act so deeply and truthfully that I
will truly die on stage.
That'll show them! I swear not to weep about
what is said about me.

She moves to the dressing room.

If it upsets me I will never show it.

She stares in the mirror and starts to make up.

35

Every show I know the company wants a reason
to replace me. One night...

She touches her burning forehead

I have a *little* fever.
Non, ça n'est pas grave, ç'est rien, I will be fine.
But they ask Marie Lloyd to take over my role.
Oh! She refuses: " Mais ç'est la rôle de Sarah" I
powder my heat, and hurry to the wings...

She moves to the wing.

...to hear them announce tonight the
performance will be Tartuffe, which I am not in!

She peeks into the auditorium.

Some people ask for their money back- from the
many fines I will be made to pay. 'Oh yes, she
will pay for her difference.'

And from that night the slander and stupid lies
took flight, like... like a cloud of wild ducks.

She strides centre stage, grandly as her denouncers.

'Did you know Sarah just stays at home in her
salon smoking cigars, surrounded by seven
savage tigers!' 'And she is *always* dressed as a
man, ready to fight so violently with anyone
that she breaks all their teeth!

'And every dawn she flies in a hot air balloon to
visit Versailles!!'

Lies, Lysiane, Lies! I only wore trousers to paint or sculpt, so I could move with the muse and my *Pumas* are tame.

LYSIANE: But… you pose for the camera. You grow your image. You know your effect.

SARAH: Oh Lysiane, to inspire other women, to grow imagination!

But the gossip gathered and I was refused party invitations. Emile Zola wrote;(*picking up a page to read)* " Ha -Ha, Sa-Rah! Not content with deeming you too thin, and declaring you insane, they now denounce your artistic expression".

Chandeliers burned without me. Although the newspapers say I was swinging on them! It was all so outrageous, I was compelled to announce.

She stands, gathering defiance.

My respect is always due La Comédie Française, cette Maison de Molière, mais… *if* the stupidities written about me scandalize Parisians and they receive me ungraciously on my return I shall send in my resignation.
En plus, if this London public condemns me I shall request of the Comédie Française to release me, so to avoid any hissing towards the stage'

She backs up to the chaise-longue and sits, spent.

LYSIANE: Et alors? What happened, Grandmère.

SARAH: Ooh, well. Much ink flowed. Everyone writes. Coquelin, Croizette: "Oh dear little Sarah, we cannot congratulate you for your rash action. When one has the good fortune and honour of belonging to the Comédie Française one must remain there until the end of one's life. Submit"

A moment. She folds the page.

> I postpone a definite decision, returning to Paris clandestine.
> But I had been home less than an hour when management arrives. Crisis talks.

She turns to her bosses, on both sides.

> But, is it my fault I am thin? That my hair is unruly?
> That I don't think as other people do? Est-ce que ç'est ma faute?
> Supposing I took arsenic for a month to swell out like a barrel, and shave my head and say *Oui* to everyone.
> You would say it was a publicity stunt!

She has chased them way.

> They call me 'Madame Révolte! And I had to get away- as far as Belgium
> ...and then, yes, I had to stay at home, until (*smiling*) I was no longer alone

LYSIANE: You had a baby, mon Papa.

Sarah moves to the floor to play with her baby boy

SARAH: Mon petit prince, Maurice! Whose father... left, leaving this little boy to defend me. When he saw a cartoon of me as a skeleton with a sponge on its skull, (*finding a page*) he ran to the newspaper office, and threw down his little glove. Apologize to ma mère! (*throwing the crumpled page*) The editor said 'I do not fight duels with 8 year old boys. Come back when you're 21'.

She stands.

My whole life, Lysiane, I'm thought 'too much' and 'too little'.

She paces then searches the floor for a particular page.

Did you find an anonymous letter?

She does, and picks it up, thrusting it out.

Voila. Vas-y, read it. N'hésites-pas

Lysiane reads, hesitantly

LYSIANE: 'My poor skeleton, you will do well to not show your horrible Jewish nose at the Comédie Française new season ceremony this week.

She glances up fearing to continue, but she does.

I fear it would serve as a target for all the potatoes now being prepared especially to throw at you.
So... Spit blood and stay in bed and think about the consequences of excessive advertisement.'

39

Sarah looks at the page, then drops it.

SARAH: I decide. I shall go to the opening ceremony.

She moves to the dressing-room to get ready.

> All the actors and actresses advance in pairs to
> the great bust of Moliere, placing palms and
> laying laurels on the pedestal.
> I am pale. No one pairs with me.

She steps slowly on 'stage'

> So I step alone slowly towards the footlights.
>
> I can't help it, my eyes glance into the monster's
> eyes, daring the pommes de terre. But instead...

Sound of applause

> They want me to stay? Perhaps my company
> wants me to too?

She looks to the wings

> I look to my fellow actors, and among them is
> my darling little sister Regina, who begged me
> to bring her, promising to be good, and she's
> clapping and jumping up and down...

She stares, horror growing.

> ...on the robe of Madame Nathalie, the dragon-
> lady soçiètaire!
> Madame Nathalie strides away and falls on her
> face.

She quickens Quelle horreur.

> She twists, grabs Regina, who is terrified, and
> hurls her hard into the stone wall. Suddenly I
> am there and I… strike the dragon down.

She takes a moment, then slowly lowers her raised arm.

> I am given 3 days to apologize.
> Bon, if Madame Nathalie apologises to Regina.
> We go home, and hear nothing.
> After 3 days I leave la Comédie Française.
> (*Deeply upset*) It was all I wanted, and now, I
> would never act again I would become my
> mother's prediction (*Horrified*) I would become
> my mother! Non, Never.
> I shall sculpt, I shall paint. I try not to faint.
> What theatre would take me now?

She sits on the chaise-longue, troubled

LYSIANE: Les Théâtre Gymnase, Renaissance, et L'Odéon

SARAH: Yes, they saved me. Until the Franco-Prussian
war came and Maman takes Jeanne, Regina, and
Maurice to Le Havre for safety.

> Someone asks 'Why didn't you go too, Sarah?'
> Because I must help turn the theatre into a
> hospital and become a nurse, my most rewarding
> role. Administering to the boy soldiers carried in
> on stretchers, to lose their limbs.

I soak up their blood, listen to their screams,
and perform on the front lines – Prussian gunfire
in the wings. Close to death.

'Grâce au ciel, mes mains ne sont point criminelles'

I feel so alone.

She is genuinely upset, wringing her hands then strikes a sudden slash at her wrists

LYSIANE: Oh, Grandmère... did you, did you try to...?

SARAH: Chèrie, if I did attempt suicide don't you think I would have succeeded?

But I did think Maman and everyone would be sorry.

LYSIANE: Including Papa's father? You never speak of my grandfather.

Sarah considers.

SARAH: You know they call it Sarah's 'spiral' when I fall to a death? That's exactly how I fell for your Grandpère.
We met at a costume ball. I went as Queen Elizabeth and he was dressed as... Hamlet. I was so surprised as his hand deepened my back and danced me onto the balcony to kiss. I slapped his cheek.

'Do not take liberties with me, Monsieur Hamlet. I am not Ophelia'.

I caught sight of our reflection; an imperious
Elizabeth and a very nervous Hamlet. He was
the first to laugh.

'The Prince of Denmark humbly begs the
Queen's pardon'.

He takes my hand, whispering 'To forgive or not
to forgive?'

Oh, I squeeze him hand 'To forgive'.

LYSIANE: Oh Grandmère, why didn't you marry him, in
real life he *was* a real Prince!

SARAH: Oui, Maman couldn't believe my luck! Imagine-
moi, une princesse! Confined to one role for the
rest of my life?

    (*she decides*) Non. I will never marry. I will work.
I will raise Maurice alone.

LYSIANE: And raise the standards on every stage.

SARAH: Well, why should women be allowed to wear hats
during a performance! Take them off so every
one of the audience can see the stage!

Sarah looks from the auditorium to the downstage edge.

    And why do we need a Prompt box? Little head
of a little man feeding us forgotten lines!

    No more, every actor must know every line!

*She strides upstage on her way to the dressing-room, then stops
and turns.*

And every actress, who has a baby, can use her
dressing room as a crèche!

She moves to the dressing room, finding her script on the floor

Oh, Maurice, please don't play with my script on
the floor! It is precious.
You know some little children grow up to be
playwrights,
See, this is written Alexandre Dumas fils, the
son! "La Dame aux Camélias".

Sarah takes the pages and wanders downstage.

Shall I show how it was a tightrope, when Paris
perceived me too personally in the role?

She 'walks' a tightrope

Just like Marguerite… 'Sarah has debts beyond
the sky
Just like Marguerite, Sarah's selling what's left
of her jewels and gold belts
Just like Margeurite, Sarah will die…in poverty.'

She falls off the tightrope

Sarah isn't royalty, after all. Non
Although I had spent like a Queen.
Because the nuns taught me it is a sin to die
rich.
But I'd promised Maurice a pony, and he
painted an empty stable, ready

I stand in our courtyard frozen, about to be
arrested.

A waif – awaiting the handcuffs.

What now? What will become of my family now?

Then I thought: 'Attends' 'Wait'

So, I went to the coffin.

She moves towards the chaise-longue.

Every cell whispering 'Wait!'

LYSIANE: For what?

SARAH: For something that will change all this.

She leans back on the chaise-longue, and crosses her arms.

It can't be far off now
For three days, I do not eat or speak or move.
The papers announce I am dying.
Until one morning...

LYSIANE: I know! A man arrives!

Sarah sees him too, and sits up

SARAH: A proper Englishman in a proper top hat.

Lysiane stands to gesture him in

LSYIANE: The impresario-extraordinaire, Monsieur Jarrett!

SARAH: La miracle! Un tour à Londres, and a grand tour en Amérique?

45

'The new world will not be cold towards you
Madame.
You will be showered with gold'.
Maurice! J'ai des bonne nouvelles!

She moves to the dressing-room to fix herself up.

Maman est invité a l'Amérique.
Oh, they will make such a fuss of me, I shall
walk into the belly of whale for publicity! But
you can come another time.

She picks petals from the vase of flowers

Let's fill the house with flowers…

*She moves centre-stage, tossing petals and finding her script pages
on the floor.*

Maurice, why is my script on the floor! What's
wrong?
I'll let you count the gold when I get back.
And I will buy your pony, yes! You will have
everything you want!
My little cowboy… Mon petit prince.

Lights change

She has changed positions, and her tone.

I won't be long, and yes I know I said I would
only do 2 or 3 tours but this 4th is because I am
spending an insane amount of money because
the gods have ordained that I adore you! Ye
gods… ç'est mon destin /
I am not acting. I am not Phedre!

And you better be grateful I am not Medea.
La role de ma vie ç'est çela de ta mère!

Lights change

She turns to the empty corner where Maurice is silent.

You are old enough to understand Maurice. If
you feel a crown of a Prince upon your head it is
because *I* buy you the best!

She continues to pick up pages.

I have to go on four more tours because it isn't
just horses you want, but carriages and clothes,
and...

She reads the pages as if they are bills

Money for drinking and gambling, and... new
duelling pistols!
Say something!
If you're angry because I am famous, well, I
give you two theatres to manage so you can be
famous too.
Please don't walk away!

Thud

She sits, sad.

LYSIANE: You abandon him.

Sarah rises, troubled, still holding all the pages she has collected.

SARAH: Non. I didn't mean...

LYSIANE: You abandon Paris.

SARAH: Non. I mean… to die here.

Sound of thud

Sarah steps forward, uneasy.

> Let's stop now, Lysiane.
> Before the three events that… nearly do kill me.
> Let's stop.

She starts to leave the stage

LYSIANE: *(quietly)* But we have to write about your mother's death.

Sarah slowly turns back, moving to the chaise-longue

SARAH: She was discovered one morning, lying on her sofa, in her pretty negligee, neglected on her lace pillow. Her hands clasping her travelling fur. She doesn't stir. Enough.

She moves to leave the stage.

LYSIANE: Non. Tell me the second event, Grandmère

SARAH: I never speak of it. Of 'her'

LYSIANE: Marie Colombier?

SARAH: Unspeakable! How did such a bad actress feign friendship with me, to gain confidences that I innocently give to inspire her! She twisted my words to the world in a book! *(she stares at the pages she holds.)* 800 pages, a best-seller!

48

LYSIANE: And Papa wanted a duel!

SARAH: But he couldn't with a woman, so he demanded
a retraction.
She laughed in his face. I was in the doorway
and heard everything.
I'd followed him on horseback, the riding whip
still in my hand

LYSIANE: Your hurled yourself at her /

SARAH: Non, I made a dramatic entrance and then I
sliced through every lie on every page, and
slashed everything else in sight.

*She has slashed the scrolled script as if Hamlet's sword, and its
pages scatter.*

LYSIANE: No one believes her book

SARAH: But they must believe yours. Vas-y, you must
keep writing.

LYSIANE: And you must keep going, Grandmère. Go on,
the third event?

SARAH: It began with a new play, Theodora

She picks up a page

LYSIANE: That Sardou wrote for you?

SARAH: Yes, I thought if I must fall in love I should do it
with a playwright. *But* Sardou also sent me a
new leading man

She hesitates, then decides to go on.

49

I was rehearsing in my garden for another tour à
Londres... repeating my lines aloud when a
strange voice replied, on cue, to each and every
one. Please, do not interrupt *(turning)*
Monsieur... *(as an aside to Lysiane)* Without
that beard he would look even younger.

LYSIANE: *(whispering back)* Jacques Damala.

SARAH: A Greek god, *(turning to 'Jacques')* You know
every scene!

She sashays around him, then back towards the chaise-longue

Voulez-vous entrer Monsieur?
'I want to make a note, of all the plays in which
you shall play opposite me: Adrienne Lecouvrir.
Please take off your hat: Ruy Blas, Hernani,
Phedre, and your coat? La Dame aux Camelias,
Frou Frou... Ah, and your veste?

She watches his every move.

L'Aventuriere, L'Etrangere and... such a fine
figure, Fedora.
Vous etes mariées? Non? Come and sit beside me.
I pour him a glass of white port. You have
talent. Consider yourself engaged. He kissed my
hand and... you may just write 'Etcetera.
Etcetera'

She rises

But he also played my Hamlet, Lysiane, and I as
Ophelia watched from the wings. My new
Hamlet. I would never slap *his* cheek.
I would marry him.

LYSIANE: But you said you would *never* marry.

SARAH: Well, this was London so if Mrs Pat could do it.
St Andrew's Church, but it was secret. Until
that night, after the show, the Illustrated
London News asked me how I like the English
"Oh, ils sont adorables. Just think, this morning
my husband and I... (*referring to Jacques beside
her*) Oui, mon mari, Monsieur Damala, we were
leaving the church when a little girl gave me a
bunch of flowers because 'you are the bride'

And she gave Jacques a sprig of heather.

She freezes. The spell is breaking.

I did not foresee the outcome.

She is truly upset

How could he go from dream lover to drug
addict, from leading man to lost soul. He
disappears for years. When I discover he's
returned to Paris, I race to an address... run up
the stairs and rush into a room... dark, dank...
and there is my Adonis...

Bare-chested, stretched out on the stone floor...
red streaks running. I pulled the needles from his

51

arm myself, but he struck at me and stuck more
in until... the day il est vraiment disparu.
I signed my name 'the widow Damala'.
I'm losing myself.

She rises, taking up a page.

I still had Theodora.

Moving to the dressing-room

In real life she was a passionate actress with a
terrible reputation I pray to her to 'please
protect me'. My nerves are shot. No opium!
Never drugs!

Je dois être naturelle! *(whispering)* Quand meme,
quand meme...

Stage lights on

Sound of thud

Sarah enters the 'stage'

> '*It occurs to me that there are always women who do
> not seem to belong to this world, because they do not
> fit into the prevailing notions of what a woman
> should be.*
> *Je n'étais pas même humain*
> *Not even human. The magic...*'

Stage lights off

I learn the dance of the seven veils, for Oscar's
Salomé and we start rehearsals. But the play is

52

banned and Oscar is imprisoned. I return to
Paris.

She picks up a page.

Then, Oscar writes begging me to play it here,
adding: PS, I *will* make it to Paris if it kills me-
and then just bury me in la çimitière Pere
Lachaise!

She stops.

He was still young. But I am in my middle act-
new roles and new lines, to join the ones on my
face, the wrinkles reminding me, spots on my
hands.

She rubs at them

Out damn spot, out I say.
All the perfumes of Arabia will not sweeten...

She holds her palms to her face, and then looks at them.

I must change my path. I take Macbeth off the
program, to break the curse!

LYSIANE: But there was a fourth event, that was worse.

SARAH: Another tour to Amerique, north and south. A
year away from debtors and doubters, and those
who wish me dead. I invite Maurice.
(*Gathering the travelling fur, she stands*) Please
come!
But he said he has better things to do. And I did
not heed the warning.

Someone had put heather in the ships saloon,
oh, just as the Scottish play is filled with
heather. I knew it brings such bad luck, but I
have to smile and greet my fellow passengers

She steps forward and falls

Then I slip... falling hard on my knee.
Already so damaged by a thousand stage falls.
And all I can hear is the sound of... applause?

She twists herself up to rise

Non, this is not another death scene, Au secours!
Docteurs!! They say it is hopeless. The urgent
treatment has to wait until I return to France.

She limps back to the safety of the chaise-longue

Your father was 21, forever fighting duels,
because
I couldn't stand up for myself. I couldn't stand.

She lays her right leg out, stiffly on the chaise-longue

One year until the treatment took effect.
And I prepare to play my first male leading role,
Lorenzaccio.

She takes the pose.

A thinker, an intellectual. A dreamer more than
fighter.
Oui, a good role model for Maurice.

Like my next role, L'Aiglon, (*standing with
effort*) the little eaglet son of Napoleon, an
unhappy prince in exile.

She bows.

Another triumph

She turns away.

Another trauma.
Regina… my sweetest sister Regina… dies.
Now there is only Jeanne and I keep her close,
but she is far gone – anger, moods and drugs.
When she dies I no longer recognized the world.
And Maurice leaves home.

She sits, lost.

Oscar returns but then he died. (*curling up on the
chaise longue*)
It seems like the End. I want to hide.

LYSIANE: Non, (*standing*) you go on to create le Theatre
Sarah Bernhardt, Châtelet, bigger than a
cathedral

SARAH: Yes, because I can hide onstage.

She steps downstage as if considering this grandest of theatres

The audience are far away… so no one can see
me too closely…
The grief of skin, the fall of cheek.
It was an illusion and a solution.
My monster's opera lorgnettes blur the lines
between life and art.

She moves to dressing-room

> And the powder blurs the lines for me

She powders her face, looking in the mirror.

LYSIANE: You become a poster girl. Rice Powder publicite

SARAH: Oui, I become the poster girl for every show. Alphonse Mucha makes much of me.

Sarah considers her face in the mirror.

> But it isn't real. We women are not allowed to be real.

A charged moment, she turns to Lysiane.

> But we must be now, chérie.

LYSIANE: What do you mean Grandmère?

SARAH: Don't you want to talk about what's really happening?

She moves towards Lysiane who deflects, picking u a page.

LYSIANE: Non. You said keep writing. We must finish before... before...

Quickly diverting and picking up a page

> Ahm, what about this?

She reads:

> "I quite see that we professional actors are really the amateurs. This is why the actors of real life

56

judge us so severely. But they are very wrong to
do so.'
Did you write this?

Sarah considers the page she holds.

SARAH: I meant real people act when they want to tell a
lie, whereas when I act I want to tell the truth.

C'était écrit en Australie.

They took me hunting for kangaroo, but deadly
snakes stalk us. One slithers into my bag. And
suddenly someone misfires. I turn to see a fallen
koala... a baby inside its blood splattered pouch.
I take it up, but...

without its mother it won't survive.
I weep. And I hear the real people say 'Oh *look*,
she must be *acting*'
Non, now I understand it is a privilege to be
present... at death.
I look up, and dare them to care.

She recovers and steps forward.

I always tell my students:
When someone is about to die, their heart is
desperate, caught between loss and love, grief
and fear.

She is now teaching her auditorium of students.

And if there is someone else in the same room,
breathing the air of the dying one's last, *their*
heart will despair too.

57

Audience assimilates actress

Come. Imagine the death of someone you love.

Don't be afraid, Lysiane.
You know, just before we die we become very
lucid, and suddenly we can speak and laugh and
live with strength... and everyone thinks oh,
she's getting better, she will live...
Don't you want to talk about it, darling? What's
really happening?

Lysiane is genuinely upset.

LYSIANE: Non. I don't... want you to see you spiral. I'm
frightened.

SARAH: Nothing to be frightened of.

Cleopatra knew she was soon to die, as I sat
draped on the throne.

She moves to sit in the chair

Stage lights

> *Give me my robe, put on my crown;*
> *I have immortal longings in me:*

I hold silence and my deadly snake from the
hunting trip.
I let it slither and *spiral* all over my body.

Her hands and body slithers seductively.

See? Nothing to be frightened of

Lysiane gives a tiny smile.

LYSIANE: Grandmère, I thought this was supposed to be *true* story

SARAH: Well, I am acting so it must be true! And what else is true is that a French Cleopatra is always more seductive than Shakespeare's. An Englishwoman wrote to complain that she could never bring her children to see me perform. 'Why, oh why, Madame Sarah, can you not play something that the whole family may enjoy! Why not play Joan Of Arc' Jeanne d'Arc, for children?

She rises, considering the idea.

Although I already knew the being-burnt-alive-by-fire scene from when I was a child.
I write back, quelle bonne idée!
This Jeanne was nothing like my sister Jeanne.
Jeanne D'Arc was always pure to her dying prayer.

Stage lights

She steps downstage as Joan Of Arc.

One life is all we have and
we live it as we believe in living it

She raises her bound hands to an invisible curtain.

Arms stretching out towards the infinite as the curtain falls.

She opens her arms.

> And then opening, like wings, to help others fly.

> And to swoon, like splendid rag dolls.
> Even when as old as me, I love to swoon.

She does, onto the chaise-longue

> By now in Paris, the public and presse expect it
> of me.
> Mais, il y a une problème. My leading men are in
> their 50s!

LYSIANE: So are you, Grandmère

SARAH: Well, that's why I want one in his 30s!

> One did came to see me, both pretending to be
> unimpressed /
> 'Alors, voulez-vous lire les lignes, s'il vous plait?'
> He studied the script as I studied him.
> (*whispering*) Quel bel Monsieur...

LYSIANE: Lou Tellegen.

SARAH: So handsome

LYSIANE: But he's in his *20s*!

SARAH: Tant mieux, even better!

> He was not the greatest actor, but he was there
> for me. On stage and even on film; *Les Amours
> de la Reine Elizabeth*. Queen Elizabeth encore.

LYSIANE: Oh yes, we must write that you were Paramount's very first film star.

SARAH: Who didn't understand film acting at first.

As Elizabeth I entered to see Lou as Essex lain on the stone… I stop, seeing him. Just like Jacques… *Oh…* It was too… much. *I* was too much!
I played to the gods, but there were no gods. *(realizing)* And there was no monster to share with.
So when we film *La Dame Aux Camellias* I play for the camera, asking the camera man, do you see the tremours of my heart? I flutter my hands, tiny truths, and the crew… cry.
Then for my epic film, *Les Mères Françaises…* I play for reality.
A new reality.

She limps. Her leg is truly bad, as she uses the sofa to help her to the dressing-room

Which is… that my leg is… much, much worse, Especially on another tour en Amérique.

Jarrett suggests we can cancel Columbus because the theatre has become unavailable and there is only a circus tent available.

I say Parfait! I shall even walk a tightrope, until I can no longer walk!

She steps to the 'stage' opening her arms as she turns a circle.

And that show was fateful, because there was nowhere to hide. I embrace the monster on every side, and every facet is seen. As the tent empties and the dust settles, the lights are like a million little stars, and there is a man, walking down from the very top row; beautifully dressed, a beautiful smile. Est-ce ç'est Maurice? Yes, Maurice!

Her eyes follow him down the stairs, flowing with emotion.

Quelle belle surprise! My son, toute seule, et tout grandit... you are so tall now

She reaches her hand to him.

He hands me a manuscript. A new play?

She opens to the first page.

Written by him, inscrit 'Pour maman'
Oh, mon petit prince, thank God you are here.

She reaches her hands out for support

I need my family now.

When we return to Paris I have to make a decision.
Either I will have my leg amputated or I shall have to kill myself.
And I shall not kill myself, because the *pain* already is killing me
Every doctor in the world has failed.
I refuse to fail. Maurice, please go and tell them.

She sits, calling after Maurice, exhausted.

I will have a wooden leg, why not?

LYSIANE: Do you want to rest now, Grandmère?

Sarah half-hears, looking out.

SARAH: Yes, I told the boy soldiers at the Odéon to rest.

They said without that theatre they felt so
alone, and so do I.

She looks deep into the auditorium

Bonsoir mon monstre bien aimé
(*whispering*)
Il y a quelqu'un?

Non, je suis seule
Living on a sofa.

She lays back.

Like my mother.

She looks up.

Do you hear me Maman?
Do you know they awarded me Chevalier of the
Legion of Honour.
How I tickled the monstre, and tamed the press.
And after I was invited back to La Comédie
Française, they created la journée Sarah
Bernhardt! And I have written 2 plays and 4
books, so I wasn't forever the loser!

She sits up, gaining strength, shifting the travelling fur.

> Bien sûr, I am still trouble, but why not trouble
> ourselves?
> Plenty of thorns have cut me to bleeding but I
> still love roses.

She looks into her palms.

> And the blood shows I am still alive.
> 'All the perfumes of Arabia…'

She holds her hands to her face.

> I can still smell your scent.
> And I sense… what do I sense?

She looks up.

> That you are still not proud?

She stands, defiant.

> You think I'm just playing games? Well, I never
> played games with you!
> I never played with dolls or a Dolls House with
> you!
> Why couldn't we play make-believe?
> Why couldn't I make you believe in me?
> That's why I need Lysiane to write the threads
> of what you didn't see.
> In me.

She moves back to the chaise-longue.

> Lysiane?

LYSIANE: Oui, Grandmère. I'm here.

SARAH: I don't understand. You look different. Are you still 13?

LYSIANE: Non, Grandmère. I am now married. To Verneuil, the playwright.

SARAH: Yes, good girl. You know when they take my leg, I shall return to America and I will present Maurice's play, and...
And if the headlines scream 'The great Sarah, the oldest person in the world, arrived in New York today'. I shall say when I'm 103 I'll show you what it is to be an old woman!'
But that's thirty years ahead, and suddenly Maurice begs me to give up the stage, and he leaves me to sleep.

Laying back

But each afternoon my dreams fill with roles reappearing. I wake with the words, but my voice is so small no one can hear me.
Who will hear me if I scream?
Because the dreams turn to nightmares: shattering stage scenery and crashing chandeliers.

She stands and steps downstage.

Enough! I am rested enough.
I want to take flight.

At the end of the balloon flight it floats over the
cemetery Pere Lachaise and I wave to the tombs
of my friends. (*whispering*) Oscar
The wine was finished so I sent the bottle
soaring into the lake at Vincennes. Swans
clapped their wings but a haunting sadness filled
the air as it drowned like an old actress...

She turns slowly steps upstage, then turns to look at the audience.

Il y a quelqu'un?

LYSIANE: Grandmere, there is a film director at the door.
He has a contract for you.

SARAH: (*She rises to the occasion, despite her frailty.*) Ah
oui. Your father doesn't know but it is for a film
called La Voyante, and a clairvoyant's a good
role for me, n'est-ce pas?
Qui vivra, verra... the future!
See? Much better to film in my salon than a
studio.

She sits, with effort.

I already have a crystal ball, and props.
And the script (*she takes a page, reads and
realizes*)
No, this is for you Lysiane. For the book.
(*reading*) 'Many of us belong to this emotional
school. We live our parts, we weep, we laugh, we
suffer and love...' Like you.
Do not be frightened. I am not.

She offers the page, and stands as Lysiane.

66

LYSIANE:　The day of Grandmère's operation we waited at the hospital and she was wheeled past us. Tiny, face white and winking. Joking...

SARAH:　I'm going, going... gone.

LYSIANE:　The doctors declared it a grand success.
Proudly saying they took her leg well above the knee to protect from infection.
She tried the prosthetic but it was too high and caused an extreme pain and not the image of a warrior she had determined to be.
So she threw the wooden leg away. And fashioned a sedan chair

She holds her arms as if to carry a throne to the dressing room

To be carried everywhere, into theatres, and dressing-rooms...

She sits

And once...

Sarah clutches the dressing table and slowly rises.

SARAH:　I balanced with my one leg, and holding onto the table.
Glancing down and see my hands are my mother's hands... holding me up,

She looks into the mirror

Quand même, Sarah, quand même...
I drew myself upwards towards her voice.

She draws herself up to stand.

> And I stand... strong.
> Inner strength, Ibsen strength.

She is very still, as Ibsen's Nora.

Stage lights

> *Yes, I have changed.*
> *I believe that I am first and foremost a human*
> *being, like you – or anyway, that I must try to*
> *become one.*
> *I know most people think as you do, Torvald...*
> *but I have duties that are... sacred*

LYSIANE: Grandmere, are you... acting? I don't know this role.

SARAH: Ç'est moi. The me, inside. A Doll's House... our Maman, *La Divine en devinant'*

She holds up all the pages from the table, offering them to Lysiane.

> Let them devour me.

Lysiane takes them, standing.

LYSIANE: We have a saying in our family, about trouble. It comes tout au coup...
But this final curtain, it fell slowly.
We no longer visited between matinees and the evening performance, no longer watching her make up in her dressing room.

The Dressing Room fades.
She wanders the stage and gathers more pages.

We are at home.

Always in white, more and more like an angel
had swooped down and dressed her in its wings.
As she reached her seventies certain things
remained amazingly young.

She continues to collect the last pages from the floor.

Her voice, her gestures, the expression of her
eyes. Her hair:
Always like an obstinate schoolgirl or a coquette.

She looks at all the pages she holds.

She re-lived and re-loved…
Because…

She looks out front.

This is no longer a story.
This is life, flashing before her eyes.

She sets the pages down as she sits on the chaise-longue.

On her 79th birthday Papa insisted she stay in
bed

SARAH: Non, I shall be returning to London, to my
corner house in Chester Square, to the English
stages where… Ellen and I are still young, not
even 80. Showtime…!

She half-rises.
Sound of thud
Stage lights
She is Phedre

> '*This feverish life I lead sustains me.*
> *A woman of the world*
> *Who…*
> *Who has a family*'
> Oui.

She reaches her hands out for them.

No one realized… I care more about my family
than my fame
Lyisane, you see, I just wanted to lead the public
to something hidden, especially in the famous
roles. Even if that hidden truth destroys a
legend.
Oscar said one day they would understand that
inside, a legend is only human.

LYSIANE: At lunch her voice is distant, a far-off whisper
towards where she was turning

Sarah looks up

SARAH: Es-tu la, Maman?
Do you want me to talk about it?
Do you want me to say, I'm sorry I wasn't with
you… à la fin?

She pulls the long fur over her, like a blanket

To place my hands on… your heart… when it…
(stopped).
Your hands… (*Seeing them*) like my hands.
They found you with your eyes open, Maman.
What were you looking for?
Moi?

> No séance I ever went to could return your
> spirit.
> But if I am La Voyante.

She turns to the Crystal Ball and tries to touch it.

She is so weak it is a supreme effort, but as she taps it, she suddenly is struck by something beyond it,

Shaken, tiny-voiced, she suddenly 'sees' her mother standing there.

> Oh! Maman...
> I... I see you.
> Tu me vois? Can you see (me)?
> Maman, you see... it's me.
> *(Reaching her hand out)*
> Ç'est Sarah, ta fille. Don't you know me?
> Why don't you recognize...?

Realising

> I am only so old because I so lived.
> Attends. J'arrive.

She turns to the tarot cards

> One more scene. I take up a tarot card

She does so and reads it, then shivers

> I'm cold. Please close the window.
> Lysiane?

She looks out.

> Il y a quelqu'un. Who's there?

MAURICE: *(V.O)* C'est moi, Maman.

Sarah sees him and reaches out a hand.

SARAH: Maurice… at last

MAURICE: (*V.O*) I've been here all the time. I've been
                writing a new play for you.

*Sarah takes a breath, touched beyond tears. Maurice's voice
continues*

                There are crowds outside.

SARAH.   I do not hear them call 'Vive Sarah'.

MAURICE: (*V.O*) Because they are praying for you.

Beat

SARAH: Playing the end before we get there, hmm? Come
                Mon petit prince… Regarde, for you, a very
                good life

She shows him a Tarot card and lets it fall.

                Who else is there?

MAURICE: (*V.O*) Journalists, maman. Shall I tell them /

SARAH: Non, no more duels.
                And in your new play, if I die, let me play a final
                game, mon petit prince
                A waiting game.

She lays back, tiny under the travelling fur, giving into it.

                The Press has tormented me enough all of my
                life…

I think we can torture it now, by making it cool
its heels a little... and wait.

*She smiles. She dies. MUSIC. Lysiane gently takes up the
manuscript and rises.*

LYSIANE: These were her last words, and her last smile.

She folds the manuscript and steps in single file downstage

The crowds grew and Paris was silent, as a
haunting sadness filled the air.
At the Theatre Sarah Bernhardt, the horse-
drawn hearse stops, to raise your coffin up.

She stops, raising the manuscript up, folded like a bound book.

And a million people follow you to Père
Lachaise. But... I imagine... in a hundred years.

*Sarah's moon light emerges. Sarah considers, as she did at the
beginning.*

SARAH: Etre ou ne pas être?
Ça, c'est la question.

And the answer...
Is always...

To be.

She opens her arms to her audience.

Quand même

Blackout.

F I N.